AF725383

Adobe Campaign Developer

By: JCM-Adobe Prep Test Preparation Group

This page is intentionally left blank.

This booklet is written independently by JCM Test Prep Group. The contents of the booklet are copyrighted by JCM Test Prep Group. The product is not endorsed by any third-party organizations. The names of the exams mentioned in this booklet are not trademarks, registered trademarks, or affiliated in any way with JCM Test Prep Group.

All rights reserved. The text of this publication, or any part thereof, may not be reproduced in any manner whatsoever without the written permission from JCM Test Prep Group. Any violation of copyright laws will be subject to possible criminal charges and/or civil penalties.

Printed in the United States of America

The author and the publisher make no warranties with respect to the correctness or completeness of the content contained in this publication and specifically disclaim all warranties whatsoever. Advice, strategies, and suggestions described may not be suitable for every case. Providing web addresses or other (information) services in this publication does not mean/imply that the author or publisher endorses information or websites. Neither the author nor the publisher shall be liable for damages arising herefrom. Websites may be infected by computer viruses. The author and publisher shall not be held responsible for any damage resulted herefrom. Websites (content) may have altered since the time the author described them in this booklet. There are no guarantees attached to the publication. The content of this publication is best practices, suggestions, common mistakes, and interpretation, and the author and the publisher are not responsible for any information contained in the publication.

Any services provided by the publication, authors, or company are with the understanding that services can be terminated with or without notice. In rendering services, the author and the publisher are not responsible for any information communicated. Users agree not to hold the service (author/publisher/company) or its employees liable for any services (information) provided or any information displayed on the website. Users release the service from any claims or any kind of damage. The author, publisher, services, and/or company are not responsible for any accuracy or legitimacy of the information provided during rendering services. There are no guarantees attached to services.

No institutions (public or private) have permission to reproduce (in any form) the contents of this publication.

This page is intentionally left blank.

Free Online Email Tutoring Services

All preparation booklets purchased directly from JCM Test Prep Group include a free four-month email tutoring subscription. Any resale of preparation booklets does not qualify for a free email tutoring subscription.

What is Email Tutoring?

Email Tutoring allows buyers to send questions to tutors via email. Buyers can send any questions regarding the exam processes, strategies, content questions, or practice questions.

JCM Test Prep Group reserves the right not to answer questions with or without reason(s).

How to use Email Tutoring?

Buyers need to send an email to jcmtestpreparationgroup@gmail.com requesting email tutoring services. Buyers may be required to confirm the email address used to purchase the preparation guide or additional information prior to using email tutoring. Once the email tutoring subscription is confirmed, buyers will be provided an email address to send questions. The four-month period will start the day the subscription is confirmed.

Any misuse of email tutoring services will result in the termination of services. JCM Test Prep Group reserves the right to terminate the email tutoring subscription at any time, with or without notice.

Comments and Suggestions

All comments and suggestions for improvements to the study guide and email tutoring services can be sent to jcmtestpreparationgroup@gmail.com.

This page is intentionally left blank.

Table of Content

Chapter 1 – About the Booklet 1

Chapter 2 – Studying Strategies 3

Chapter 3 – Test Taking Strategies 7

Chapter 4 - Reducing Anxiety Strategies 15

Chapter 5 – Guessing Strategies 19

Chapter 6 – Strategies To Decide Between Two Answers 21

Chapter 7 – Systematic Approach To Answering Questions 23

This page is intentionally left blank.

Chapter 1 – About the Booklet

Importance of Test-Taking Strategies

Effective test-taking strategies are important during standardized exams, as they can significantly impact performance and outcomes. These strategies not only help in managing time efficiently but also aid in comprehending and tackling the diverse formats of questions presented. Skilled test takers understand the value of techniques such as strategic guessing, the process of elimination, and prioritizing questions based on difficulty level. Moreover, they recognize the significance of staying calm and focused amidst the pressure of timed assessments. Ultimately, mastering these strategies not only enhances test scores but also promotes critical thinking skills essential for academic and professional success.

What is included in this study guide booklet?

This study guide booklet only contains test-taking strategies for the Adobe Campaign Developer exam. Over 70 strategies are included to help you pass the Adobe Campaign Developer exam. The booklet will cover the following topics:

- Study Strategies
- Test Taking Strategies
- Reducing Anxiety Strategies
- Guessing Strategies
- Strategies To Decide Between Two Answers
- Systematic Approach To Answering Questions

This page is intentionally left blank.

Chapter 2 – Studying Strategies

With any standardized exam, studying smart and right are the key aspects to ensuring your success on the exam. Studying smart allows you to obtain relevant information in a timely manner, which contributes to your success on the exam. Moreover, studying right and smart reduces frustration and anxiety, which are factors that impact scores. The following are studying tips that are extremely useful in your journey to passing the Adobe Campaign Developer exam.

Studying Strategy 1 – Study the Right Materials

When studying, using the right materials is a critical aspect of increasing the chances of passing. Remembering and understanding the right content and exam questions will help students be successful on the exam. Many students buy 1000s of practice questions and 1000s of flashcards, which have nothing to do with the real exam. The human brain is capable of only remembering so much information, especially under time conditions. The best approach is to use the materials and content on the official test website. Or, go with a test preparation company that only specializes in the Adobe Campaign Developer exam and no other exams.

Studying Strategy 2 – Dedicate Studying Time

Devoting enough studying time is critical for retention and overall readiness of the exam. Students are very busy with school, jobs, and/or family, so finding time to study can be a challenge. The best approach is to set a time of the day to devote only to studying. Studying at the same time every day or every other day will keep your schedule consistent. This will prevent you from deferring studying.

Studying Strategy 3 – Avoid Memorizing Everything

Many students have the mindset to memorize everything to be ready for the exam. No one can memorize everything; that is impossible. We recommend that students memorize what is absolutely critical but focus more on reviewing as opposed to memorizing. For example, if you read a chapter in a book, then 1-2 weeks later, you want to go back and look at the chapter again. The more you look at the content or practice questions, the higher the chances you will recall the information. Memorizing everything can be overwhelming and frustrating, so the recommendation is to read, understand, and review.

Studying Strategy 4 – Effective Way to Use Flashcards

Students have a tendency to just go into making a lot of flashcards; however, some thought needs to be put into developing flashcards. When used properly, flashcards can be a very helpful tool in the studying process. The best approach is to make flashcards of information you have difficulty recalling or difficulty understanding. We highly discourage making hundreds or thousands of flashcards as that requires too much effort, but that approach can also be ineffective.

Studying Strategy 5 – Study With a Focused Mind

Passing the exam is a critical aspect of reaching aspirations and dreams, so many students will get frustrated and worried about passing. While studying, the best approach is to be focused and positive. Negative distractions while studying are just as bad as distractions during the exam.

Studying Strategy 6 – Focus on Strengths and Weaknesses

You want to focus on weak areas, but you also want to focus on stronger areas while studying. If you have been consistently weak in certain areas, your chances of getting more questions correct in those weak areas are less. You have a higher chance of getting more questions correct in stronger areas if you devote more time studying in those stronger areas. So, don't forget to study strong areas.

Studying Strategy 7 – Second Guessing

Students tend to second guess themselves on the exam all the time. While studying, keep track of the questions you second-guess. This will allow you to see which answer is correct: the first or the second. This will tell you the approach you need to take when completing the real exam.

Studying Strategy 8 – Ask Friends for Insight

Ask your friends who have taken the exam which resources were helpful. Or, ask your friends about topics that were on the exam so you can study those topics.

General Study Tips

1. Don't study sitting on top of a bed.
2. Keep your phone switched off while studying.
3. Get everything (materials, paper, pencil, etc.) needed prior to studying.
4. If you are studying for long periods, take breaks.
5. Find a quiet place to study with little distractions.

This page is intentionally left blank.

Chapter 3 – Test Taking Strategies

The Adobe Campaign Developer can be very challenging to complete, so good test-taking strategies are critical to increase your chances of getting the questions correct. Remember, test-taking strategies are not the magic answer to getting all questions correct; they are meant to increase your chances of getting the questions correct. With the pressure of completing the exam under time constraints, you can gain knowledge on test-taking strategies to smoothly finish the exam without getting stressed during the middle of the test. Below are test-taking strategies that can be applied to the Adobe Campaign Developer exam.

Test Taking Strategy 1 – Focus on the Best Answer

Answer choices that are true are not necessarily always correct. When taking the exam, you want to focus on the best answer as opposed to true statements.

Test Taking Strategy 2 – Broadest, Most Comprehensive Answer

When unsure about the answer, you want to look for the answer choice that includes all the other answer choices, which is referred to as the "umbrella effect."

Test Taking Strategy 3 – Keep Audience in Mind

If the question mentions the grade level or age, eliminate answer choice(s) that are/are not grade or age-appropriate.

Test Taking Strategy 4 – Understand the Question

You need to completely read and understand the question before looking at the answer choices. In fact, after understanding the question, you need to think of the answer without looking at the options. After that, you can look at the options and select the answer. If the answer that you thought of was one of the options, that is the one to select.

Test Taking Strategy 5 – Focus on the Timing of Event

Many students look at keywords such as most, best, least, or first, but they don't look at keywords related to the timing of events. When reading the question, you want to pay attention to when the event is taking place. Knowing when the event is taking place can help you eliminate answer choices or select the correct answer.

Test Taking Strategy 6 – Negative Words

Pay close attention to negative words (ex., not, never, except, least, cannot, won't, don't, no, contraindicated, or avoid) or negative phrases (all the following except) in the stem of the question. In this type of question, a correct answer may reflect something that is false.

Test Taking Strategy 7 – Exam Based on Textbook Information and Practices

Some individuals have years of experience working in the field. The exam is based on textbook practices as opposed to the real world. When selecting answers, you want to think about the studying that you did and not your experience. It is important to be aware of this when answering questions with the word "best." Also, this strategy is helpful to keep in mind when dealing with both content and situational questions.

Test Taking Strategy 8 – Use Time Wisely

Don't spend too much time on one question. You should attempt to maintain a pace that will allow you to devote enough time to each question. If you find yourself rereading or having difficulty with a given question, select an answer and move forward. Spending too much time on one question may cost you the opportunity to answer other questions that you can actually answer.

Test Taking Strategy 9 – Time Is Running Out

If you find yourself in a position where you have many questions left to go and not enough time, you want to start reading fast. Also, don't spend any more time on questions you are doubtful about. In the last few minutes, you want to start guessing on the remaining questions.

Test Taking Strategy 10 – Be Careful in Changing Answers

Once you have selected an answer, try to avoid changing your answers. Only change your answer if you have a strong reason to make the change. Or, you have encountered information from other questions on the test that warrants you to change the answer.

Test Taking Strategy 11 – Marking Questions for Review

If the exam allows you to mark questions for review, be careful not to mark too many questions for review. In fact, try to avoid marking questions for review that you have no clue about; no need to waste time reviewing those questions.

Test Taking Strategy 12 – Unknown Words

If you encounter a word you do not know in the question, do not panic. Also, don't quickly jump to the conclusion that you will get the question wrong. Read and understand the overall question.

Test Taking Strategy 13 – Avoid Looking At Patterns

Do not look for a pattern in the answers. If you have already selected option A for several questions in a row, do not be reluctant to choose option A again if you think that it is the correct answer.

Test Taking Strategy 14 – Look for Synonyms

Most likely, exam writers will not use a word from the question in the correct answer choice; that is too easy. However, exam writers might use a synonym in the answer choice that is linked back to a word in the question. The key is to pay attention to synonyms.

Test Taking Strategy 15 – Use the Computer Mouse

To keep yourself focused and prevent yourself from misreading the question on the computer, you may want to move the mouse under the words as you read.

Test Taking Strategy 16 – Look for Similarities and Groupings

You can look for similarities and groupings in answer choices and the one-of-a-kind key idea in multiple-choice responses. For example, if all the options are related to outdoor activity except for one option, which is related to indoors, then perhaps the correct answer can be the one related to indoors.

Test Taking Strategy 17 – First Action

When questions have the word first or initial, you have to be careful as more than one answer choice might be true. In such questions, selecting the response with the highest priority is important.

Test Taking Strategy 18 – False Statements

If any part of the answer choice is false, then the entire statement is false.

Test Taking Strategy 19 – Keep It Simple

Sometimes, the obvious answers are overlooked, so keep it simple by not overlooking them or reading too much into questions and answer choices.

Test Taking Strategy 20 – Use True and False Approach

If you are unsure of how to eliminate answer choices, if possible, turn options into true-or-false responses in order to narrow down to two possible options.

Test Taking Strategy 21 – No Options Look Correct

Occasionally, you might encounter a question where none of the answer choices look correct. First, you want to determine if the question has a negative or positive tone and then find an answer choice that reflects the tone of the question. Or, if the question is about students, think about which option will be the most beneficial to the students.

Test Taking Strategy 22 – Similar Answer Choices

Sometimes, if two options are extremely similar, neither can be the answer.

Test Taking Strategy 23 –Reasons For Correct and Incorrect Answers

To increase your chances of getting the question correct, make sure that you have a reason as to why the answer is correct. Moreover, have a reason why the other options are incorrect.

Test Taking Strategy 24 – Completely Addresses The Question

Ask yourself whether the option you are considering completely addresses the question. If the option is only partly true or is true only under certain narrow conditions, then it is likely not the right answer.

Test Taking Strategy 25 – Avoid Making Assumptions

If you have to make an assumption to justify that the answer is correct, that option most likely is not the correct answer. Even if you make an assumption in order for the answer to be true, ask yourself whether this assumption is obvious enough that most test takers will make. If not, don't select that answer.

Test Taking Strategy 26 – Tricky and Deceptive Questions

Some of the test questions can be tricky with two similar right answers. However, the test makers are not purposely writing a question intended to be extremely deceptive. If you suspect that a question is a trick item, make sure you are not reading too much into the question.

Test Taking Strategy 27 – Familiar and Difficult Words

Don't select an answer just because it is the only one with the words you recognize. Exam writers do not put fake words on the test. If you only recognize the words in one option, make sure it is correct and really addresses the question before you choose it. Also, you want to make an effort to dissect difficult words; notice prefixes and suffixes for clues.

Test Taking Strategy 28 – Careful With 100% Qualifiers

On the exam, some answer choices might include 100% qualifiers, such as always, all, everyone, none, never, ever, or must. These words imply that there are no exceptions. There are very few instances in which a correct answer is that absolute, so caution has to be taken when these words are included in the answer choices. If you select an answer choice that has a 100% qualifier, you need to be 100% sure the answer is correct. In addition, you also need to have a reason why the other options are incorrect.

Test Taking Strategy 29 – Qualifiers That Fall Between Extremes

Some answer choices might include qualifiers that fall between extremes. Some examples include seldom, sometimes, often, frequently, most, many, few, some, usually, generally, and ordinarily. These answer choices are usually true. Moreover, if you narrow the choices down to two options and one of the options has one of these qualifiers, that option is likely the one to select.

Test Taking Strategy 30 – Types of Questions

On the exam, there are typically three types of questions, which are:

1. questions, you know the correct answer with nearly 100% certainty
2. questions you think you know but are debating between 2 answers
3. questions you absolutely do not know at all

When taking the exam, you don't want to spend too much time on the third type of questions. If you see a question you absolutely do not know, simply guess and move forward. The chances of getting the third type of questions correct are low, so you do not want to waste time on those questions. Plus, your anxiety can increase if you spend too much time on the third type of question. Focus on questions that you are more likely going to get correct. If time allows, you want to go back over the second type of questions.

Test Taking Strategy 31 – Avoid Thinking About Previous Exam Attempts

If you are a repeat test taker, when taking the exam, do not think about your previous attempts. Do not think about what you put as answers in the previous attempts. If you do, your mind will start playing tricks on you, which will impact your score negatively.

This page is intentionally left blank.

Chapter 4 - Reducing Anxiety Strategies

Anxiety is the apprehension over an upcoming event. Anxiety can increase heart rate, cause lack of sleep, or poor concentration levels. Test anxiety increases with increased importance, increased likelihood of failing, test proximity, and feeling more unprepared. Having anxiety has played a significant part in many individuals retaking the exam multiple times. Reducing anxiety is a great factor in having a focused mindset and completing the test in a timely manner. Below are strategies for reducing and managing anxiety.

Importance of Reducing Anxiety Strategy 1 – Be Prepared

Individuals have anxiety because they are not fully ready for the exam. One of the main aspects of reducing anxiety is to study right; you want to be prepared and organized in your studying. Also, you want to practice the right questions and the right content. Knowing what is on the exam and learning about the exam is one of the key aspects to reducing your anxiety.

Importance of Reducing Anxiety Strategy 2 – Get a Good Night Sleep

Having a good night's sleep is critical to support you in reducing anxiety, along with establishing a focused mindset. If possible, several days prior to the exam, you want to get in the habit of getting enough sleep. Most importantly, the night before the exam, you want to have a full rest.

Importance of Reducing Anxiety Strategy 3 – Eating Well

Eating healthy days before the exam is critical to support you on your exam date. Most importantly, you want to have a good meal prior to taking the exam to ensure you have the energy to complete the exam.

Importance of Reducing Anxiety Strategy 4 – Do Unrelated Activities

For those with high-level anxiety, the recommendation is to do unrelated activities that are fun and distracting the day before the exam. You want to plan your studying to be completed prior to the exam date and take one day off to relax. Do something away from your studying materials. Meditating or spending time with friends the day before the exam is excellent to undertake.

Importance of Reducing Anxiety Strategy 5 – Be Positive

Throughout the studying process, you want to have a positive mindset. This will allow you to consume knowledge and retain information. It is absolutely important to be positive days before the exam, right before the exam, and during the exam.

Importance of Reducing Anxiety Strategy 6 – Techniques to Reduce Anxiety

To reduce anxiety, practice guided imagery, visualization of passing the test, or breathing techniques. While taking the test, if you have high anxiety, take a short 1-2 minute break to just relax the brain. Or, take a long, slow breath in through your nose.

Importance of Reducing Anxiety Strategy 7 – Avoid Negative Talks

Do not engage in negative talks with anyone before the test. Don't talk to other individuals about being nervous or not studying properly.

Importance of Reducing Anxiety Strategy 8 – Turn Negative Thinking into Positive Thinking

If you have very high anxiety and start thinking negatively, eliminate negative thoughts of self-talk by replacing them with a positive affirmation, such as "I am super ready," "I can do this," or "I studied a lot, so I am ready."

Importance of Reducing Anxiety Strategy 9 – Don't Worry About Other Test Takers

You do not need to worry about other students who finish the test before you do. If you see someone leaving the room within 1 hour of starting the test, do not panic or think about the student leaving so early.

Importance of Reducing Anxiety Strategy 10 – Sit in a Comfortable Area

If possible, you want to sit where you feel the most comfortable. If you have high anxiety, try to avoid sitting by the door or window, as these can be distracters.

Importance of Reducing Anxiety Strategy 11 – Avoid Panicking

Do not panic if you encounter 3-5 questions in a row that you do not know. The key is to try your best and think positively. If you start panicking, that can impact you on other questions as you complete the test.

Importance of Reducing Anxiety Strategy 12 – Mock Practice Test

You want to take a mock practice test under the same conditions as you will on the exam date. Make sure to time yourself and have no distractions as you take the mock test.

This page is intentionally left blank.

Chapter 5 – Guessing Strategies

When taking multiple-choice exams, the majority of test takers will have to guess at one point. Naturally, knowing the correct answer is the best approach. However, you can be in a situation where you have to guess. There is no 100% guarantee that the guess will be correct, but there are ways to improve your odds of getting the question correct by knowing some effective guessing strategies.

Guessing Strategy 1 – Maximizing Your Score

Let's say you encounter questions you absolutely do not have any clue as to what the questions are asking. These questions are questions you do not understand at all. For those questions, you will be forced into guessing. The key to maximizing your score is to select the same guess for all questions you absolutely do not know. Using the same letter guess only applies to questions you absolutely do not know and cannot eliminate any answer choices. If you can eliminate an answer choice, then you should not use this approach. By using the same guess each time on questions you absolutely do not know, your chances of getting a few extra points increase. Again, this strategy only works if you have zero clue what the question is asking.

Guessing Strategy 2 – Avoid 100% Qualifiers In Guessing

Don't ever guess an option that has 100% qualifiers, such as always, all, everyone, none, never, ever, or must.

Guessing Strategy 3 – Avoid Exaggerated or Complex Answers

When guessing, you want to avoid exaggerated or complex answers, as those are generally false.

Guessing Strategy 4 – Strongest Answer

When guessing, select the option that you feel is more closely related to the question being asked. Or, select the answer choice that you can link back to your studying.

Guessing Strategy 5 – General Responses

When guessing, you want to avoid selecting general responses, as those are typically not the correct answers.

Guessing Strategy 6 – First Instinct

You can always select the answer choice that first caught your eye.

Guessing Strategy 7 – Two Contradictory Options

When you do not know the best answer and need to guess, look for two contradictory options. One of those options can be the correct answer.

Guessing Strategy 8 – Wording of Question

Just because an option has a word that the question statement includes does not make that option the correct answer. In fact, when guessing, you do not want to pick an answer choice only because it has a word from the question.

Chapter 6 – Strategies To Decide Between Two Answers

The Adobe Campaign Developer exam does include many questions, and there are two options that can be the one correct answer. Many students complain that they don't know how to narrow down to the one correct answer. Others complain that their anxiety increases when they encounter questions with two similar answers. Many of the study guidebooks or preparation sites do not address how to approach questions with two possible correct answers. Below are some strategies to help determine the correct answer when you have narrowed it down to two options. You want to use these strategies in the order presented.

Strategy 1 – Think in Terms of Why One Option is Incorrect

When you have narrowed down to two options, try to think in terms of why one might not be the answer. If you can think of a reason, then that option might not be correct.

Strategy 2 – Contextual Clues

You want to understand the context of the question. More than one answer may look correct, but one will fit the context better.

Strategy 3 – Look at Qualifiers

If you narrow the choices down to two options and one of the options has one of the qualifiers that fall between extreme qualifiers, that option is likely the one to select.

Strategy 4 – Think About Students' Best Interest

When the question is about a student, you want to pick the answer choice that will impact the student in a positive manner or support the student in a greater manner. This is a strategy that typically works when the question has a positive or neutral tone.

Strategy 5 – First Action To Take

If you are down to two answer choices, think of which option needs to be taken first, regardless of whether the question asks for the first action.

Strategy 6 – Use the Umbrella Effect

When you are down to two answer choices, think about the umbrella effect. See if one option can be completed within the other option.

Strategy 7 - Vividly Imagining

If you are unable to choose between two answers, try vividly imagining the two answer choices. If you are like most people, you will often feel that one of the answers is right. Trust your feelings.

Chapter 7 – Systematic Approach To Answering Questions

The following are suggested steps for answering situational questions:

1. Read and understand the question.

2. If you do not understand the question at all, use the strategies presented in Chapter 5. You can also look at the answer choices.

3. If you do understand the question, think of what likely might be the answer without looking at the options.

4. Read each option carefully.

5. If one of the options is what you thought in Step 3, select that answer.

6. Otherwise, eliminate all false statements.

7. Select the answer you believe to be correct.

8. If you have narrowed it down to two options, use the strategies presented in Chapter 6.

9. The recommendation is to only change your answer if you have a strong justification to make the change.

The following are suggested steps for answering content (factual) questions:

1. Read and understand the question.
2. If you do not understand the question at all, use the strategies presented in Chapter 5. You can also look at the answer choices.
3. Otherwise, read each option carefully.
4. If you see the correct answer or are over 80% confident in the answer, select that option.
5. If you are debating between two answers, go with your gut on which is the correct answer or the first option that caught your eye.
6. The recommendation is to only change your answer if you have a strong justification to make the change.

www.ingramcontent.com/pod-product-compliance
Lightning Source LLC
LaVergne TN
LVHW022325200926
848481LV00004B/1440
* 9 7 9 8 3 4 9 4 8 1 7 1 0 *